Watch It Grow

Watch a Pumpkin Grow

by Kirsten Chang

Bullfrog
Books

Ideas for Parents and Teachers

Bullfrog Books let children practice reading informational text at the earliest reading levels. Repetition, familiar words, and photo labels support early readers.

Before Reading

- Discuss the cover photo. What does it tell them?

- Look at the picture glossary together. Read and discuss the words.

Read the Book

- "Walk" through the book and look at the photos. Let the child ask questions. Point out the photo labels.

- Read the book to the child, or have him or her read independently.

After Reading

- Prompt the child to think more. Ask: Do you like carving pumpkins or eating pumpkin pie? Can you explain how pumpkins grow?

Bullfrog Books are published by Jump!
5357 Penn Avenue South
Minneapolis, MN 55419
www.jumplibrary.com

Library of Congress Cataloging-in-Publication Data

Names: Chang, Kirsten, 1991– author.
Title: Watch a pumpkin grow / by Kirsten Chang.
Description: Minneapolis, MN: Jump!, [2019]
Series: Watch it grow | Includes index.
Identifiers: LCCN 2018020642 (print)
LCCN 2018029588 (ebook)
ISBN 9781641282635 (ebook)
ISBN 9781641282611 (hardcover: alk. paper)
ISBN 9781641282628 (pbk.)
Subjects: LCSH: Pumpkin—Juvenile literature.
Classification: LCC SB347 (ebook)
LCC SB347 .C43 2019 (print) | DDC 635/.62—dc23
LC record available at https://lccn.loc.gov/2018020642

Editor: Jenna Trnka
Designer: Michelle Sonnek

Photo Credits: Alex Coan/Shutterstock, cover; redmal/iStock, 1; Sean Locke Photography/Shutterstock, 3; Arthur Eugene Preston/Shutterstock, 4; View Stock/SuperStock, 5; Regesha Iryna/Shutterstock, 6–7; FotoDuets/Shutterstock, 8, 22tl; Madlen/Shutterstock, 9 (soil), 23bm; Ilya Akinshin/Shutterstock, 9 (watering can); Volodymyr Nikitenko/Shutterstock, 10–11, 22mr; Anongluckruttana/Shutterstock, 12–13, 22br, 23tm; Grigoriy Pil/Shutterstock, 14–15, 22bl, 23br; Elena Masiutkina/Shutterstock, 16–17; Lisa F. Young/Shutterstock, 18; KidStock/Blend Images/SuperStock, 19, 23tl; Bondar Illia/Shutterstock, 20–21; Rebell/Shutterstock, 22ml, 23bl; Denis Pogostin/Shutterstock, 23tr; Artem Samokhvalov/Shutterstock, 24.

Printed in the United States of America at Corporate Graphics in North Mankato, Minnesota.

Table of Contents

From a Seed

It is fall.

We are at a pumpkin patch.

We each
pick one!

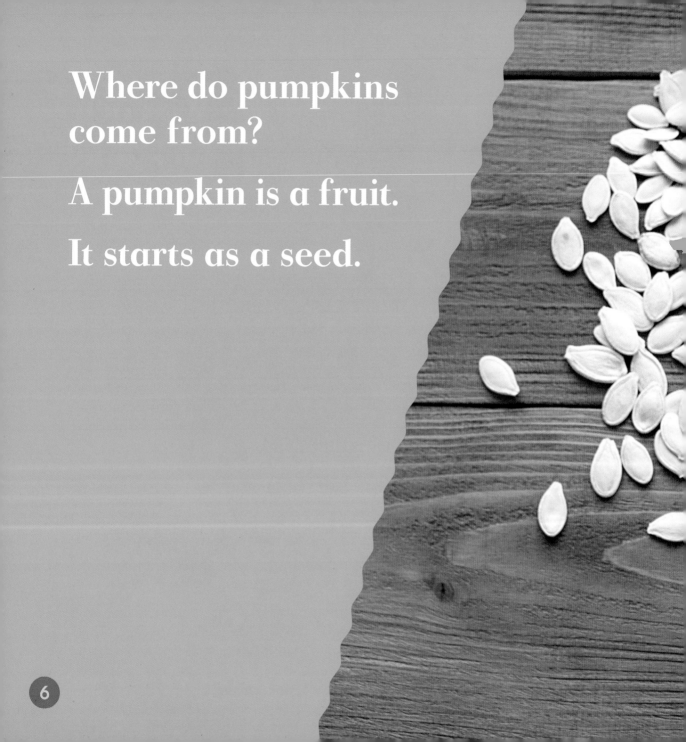

Where do pumpkins come from?

A pumpkin is a fruit.

It starts as a seed.

fruit

seed

A farmer
plants a seed
in the ground.

The soil must
be warm.

It should be rich.

The seed
needs water.

plant

A plant grows.
It gets sunlight.

It grows flowers.

Bees buzz around.

They pollinate
the plant.

This helps it grow.

bee

flower

13

vine

Pumpkins grow
on a vine.

It takes a
few months.

When they are ripe, farmers cut them from the vine.

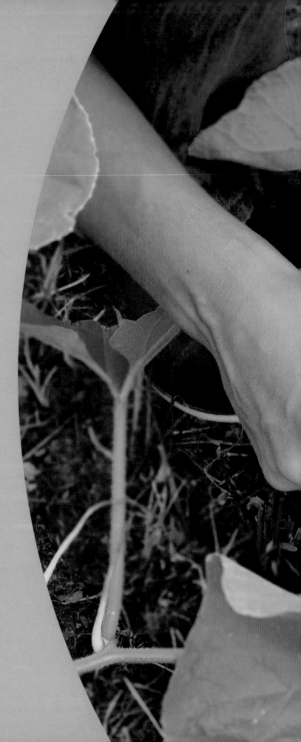

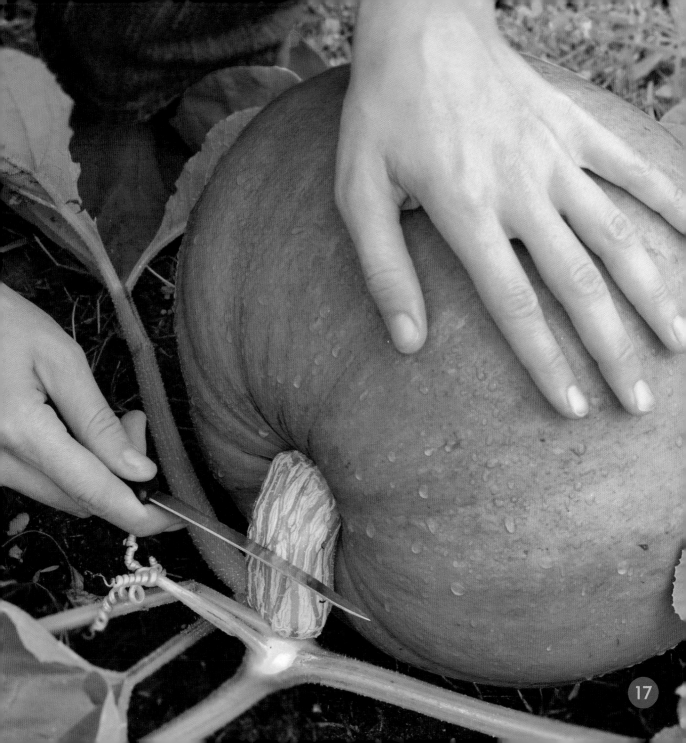

pumpkin
pie

**Pumpkins go
in pies. Yum!**

We carve them. Fun!

19

We love pumpkins!

21

Life Cycle of a Pumpkin

How does a pumpkin grow?

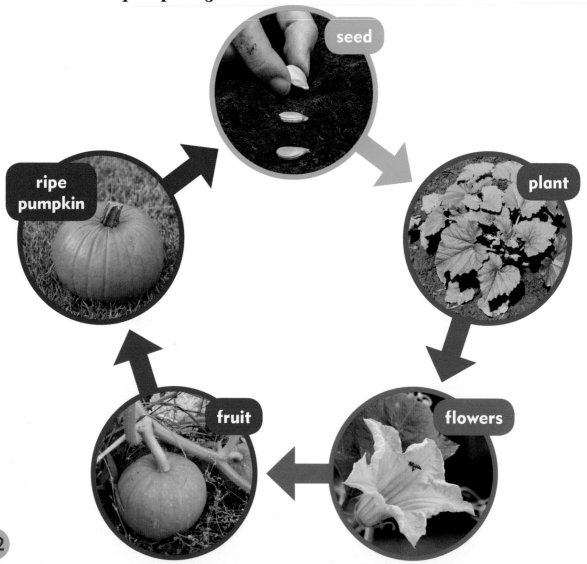

seed

plant

flowers

fruit

ripe
pumpkin

Picture Glossary

carve
To cut carefully into slices or shapes.

pollinate
To give a plant pollen so that it can grow.

rich
Productive and fertile; rich soil is good for growing plants.

ripe
Fully grown.

soil
Another word for dirt.

vine
A plant with a long, twisting stem that grows along the ground or climbs.

Index

To Learn More

Learning more is as easy as 1, 2, 3.

1) Go to www.factsurfer.com

2) Enter "watchapumpkingrow" into the search box.

3) Click the "Surf" button to see a list of websites.

With factsurfer.com, finding more information is just a click away.